Recipes of a
Pitchfork Ranch
Hostess

Recipes of a
Pitchfork Ranch
Hostess

The Culinary Legacy of
Mamie Burns

Cathryn A. Buesseler
and
L. E. Anderson

Foreword by
Georgia Mae Ericson

Texas Tech University Press

This book was set in **Americana BT and Giddyup**. The paper used in this book meets the minimum requirements of ANSI/NISO Z39.48-1992 (R1997). ∞

Printed in the United States of America

Design by Brandi Price
Cover photo of Mamie Sypert Burns courtesy of the Burns Hamilton family

Library of Congress Cataloging-in-Publication Data
    Buesseler, Cathryn A.
      Recipes of a Pitchfork Ranch hostess : the culinary
    legacy of Mamie Burns / Cathryn A. Buesseler and L. E.
    Anderson ; foreword by Georgia Mae Ericson.
        p. cm.
    Includes bibliographical references and index.
     ISBN 0-89672-475-1 (pbk. : alk. paper)
     1. Cookery--Texas. 2. Burns, Mamie Sypert, 1896-
    1982. I. Anderson, L. E., 1950- II. Pitchfork Ranch (Tex.)
    III. Title.
     TX715 .B949 2002
     641.59764--dc21

                    2001005095

02 03 04 05 06 07 08 09 01 / 9 8 7 6 5 4 3 2 1

Texas Tech University Press
Box 41037
Lubbock, Texas 79409-1037 USA

1-800-832-4042
ttup@ttu.edu
www.ttup.ttu.edu

Contents

Breads

Salads, Relishes, & Condiments

Meats

Vegetables

Desserts

Beverages

Miscellaneous

Contents
viii

Menus & Special Occasions

Foreword

The Joy of Dining with Mamie

The joy of being invited to one of the special Pitch-fork Ranch meals for visiting dignitaries or the St. Louis owners did not reach as far as my Connecticut address. On my return to my native Texas, I did have the joy of meeting Mamie Sypert Burns and becoming an audience for the vivid description of these fabulous meals and recipes, as well as her partnership in the operation of the "Forks." I was especially interested in her entertaining because my career years had been spent in the food industry.

Visiting with Mamie in her retirement apartment was reminiscent of the pasture's beauty, with broomweed arrangements throughout her abode. While on the Pitchfork Ranch, Mamie entertained ladies from Lub-bock with afternoons of bridge and tea. Sometimes she took these guests out to the pastures to gather armloads of broomweed to decorate their city homes. Mamie shared the excitement of discovery when she opened her trunk, filled with mementoes of her life on the renowned Pitchfork Ranch. Her journals and sto-ries later became the manuscript for her book *This I Can Leave You,* dedicated to her grandchildren Burns Hamilton and Anne Hamilton Fabian and published by Texas A&M Press in 1986.

The highlight of our friendship occurred in Hereford, Texas, June 1981, when I participated in the cere-mony inducting Mamie Sypert Burns into the National Cowgirl Museum and the Western Heritage Hall of Fame. Mamie now is one of 153 honorees in a twenty-one-million-dollar museum located in the cultural district of Fort Worth, Texas. The Hall of Fame yearbook contains Mamie's picture and this tribute: "Mamie Sypert Burns, Texas Western Heritage. Mamie brought her proper Houston upbringing to the famous Pitchfork Ranch on the plains of West Texas. She added a woman's touch to a place of numerous hardships. Mamie was the first gracious hostess and could perform any job inside the house or out on the range. Always serving a hot cup of coffee, her house epitomized the hospitable spirit of the West."

Being a part of this publication is an honor to an old friend.

Georgia Mae Smith Ericson, 2002

Introduction

Mamie and D Burns began their twenty-three-year love affair with the Pitchfork Land and Cattle Company in 1942 when D became the fifth manager of the Texas 165,000-acre spread, the 35,000-acre ranch in Wyoming, and the 4,000-acre summer pasture in Kansas. Mamie gave the location of the Pitchfork Ranch as "the big pasture part of Texas in the short grass country, 200 miles south of Amarillo, 83 miles east of Lubbock, 100 miles north of Abilene, and 285 miles due west of Neiman-Marcus." Today the Forks remains under the control of the St. Louis families who financially backed Daniel Gardner in 1881 when he bought the first 80,000 acres—still the core of the ranch—and 2,500 steer wearing the Pitchfork brand.

In many ways, the Pitchfork Ranch operates today just as it did in Dan Gardner's day. Much of the cattle work is still done on horseback, and branding has changed little in the last 120 years. The chuck wagon still goes out to the cowboys working the pastures, though now more often the food is prepared in the chuckhouse kitchen and transported by pickup truck. The hands who eat at headquarters still find the chuckhouse table loaded with their preferred three Bs: Beef, Beans, and Biscuits, plus several side dishes and desserts.

The residents of the Big House, or headquarters house, are still as generous with their hospitality as was Dan Gardner. Mamie Burns certainly enjoyed setting a bountiful table for her guests, as her recipes and her reminiscences indicate. In the notes Mamie left, she tells us, "On the Ranch I cooked more and enjoyed it less than anyone alive, I guess." Nonetheless, in this, her cookbook, Mamie shows her enthusiasm for preparing wonderful food to enjoy with treasured friends, family, and Ranch visitors. Mamie did realize the quality of her cooking when she said, "I may never make the ranks of the gourmet cookbooks, but on the Pitchfork, by the Williams [family], I rated A-1. They told me so."

William Curry Holden, speaking at D's last rites on October 11, 1977, summed up the welcome the Pitchfork ranch offered: "Distinguished visitors came from many states and foreign countries to inspect and buy cattle and horses. With Mamie, gracious lady that she is, as hostess, hospitality at the Pitchfork rivaled that of the Old South before the Civil War."

This book will give you a taste of Mamie's special dishes enjoyed by family and visitors as well as a glimpse of West Texas ranch life as it was lived by Mamie and D Burns, cowboys, and other ranch hands. Were you to visit the Forks today, you would encounter similar lifestyle and hospitality.

Chef L. E. Anderson, CEC, has made and served a number of these recipes with great success. Chef Anderson is in charge of the operation of Skyviews restaurant in Lubbock, Texas, which is the practical teaching facility for Texas Tech University students enrolled in Restaurant, Hotel, and Institutional Management (RHIM). Chef Anderson was excited about Mamie's recipes and was pleased to comment on many of them, rating his favorites with ✭ for very good and ✭✭ for extra special.

Mamie once wrote, "I have a shelf devoted entirely to cookbooks. They range from *Life*'s elegantly illustrated beauties to humble paperbacks on chuck wagon foods. A great many have notes scribbled on the first pages. A few of the latter, to which I have contributed, are Alma Schmit's and Ace Reed's, the famous cartoonist. The one that means the most to me says, 'Here are some recipes just a little different to a Mother who is the same. [signed by Mamie's daughter] Babe, Mother's Day 1946.' Some other day I may write one myself."

And here it is!

Cathryn A. Buesseler, Editor
Lubbock, Texas 2002

D in his office, hard at work on ranch business. Photo courtesy of the Burns Hamilton family.

How to Read a Culinary Legacy: A Cautionary Tale

The recipes that follow appear just as Mamie Burns jotted them into her personal loose-leaf recipe book. They include the brand names Mamie preferred and sometimes the prices that she paid for ingredients. In many cases she listed only the ingredients, because to this experienced cook, the methods were second nature. As an aid to the less knowledgeable, pan sizes and cooking temperatures have been suggested by Chef Anderson.

Not to discourage you from making any of these recipes, but as a word of caution—Mamie's grand-daughter-in-law says that Mamie was always glad to give out her recipes, but she frequently left out an ingredient. She always acted surprised when she was told, "I followed your recipe, but mine didn't turn out quite the same." For example, the pressed chicken recipe calls for cornmeal only, but in Mamie's description of her mother's pressed chicken there is flour added. There is no way to tell what Mamie may have omitted from these written recipes, but nevertheless, you will find they will all add to your eating pleasure. Be encouraged to add, or subtract, a seasoning or alter the amount of an ingredient to make the dish more your own and to your own taste.

Do not despair if you cannot find Brer Rabbit molasses or a five-cent can of evaporated milk. Another brand will do, and prices have risen since Mamie's day. I recall the time my mother sent me the recipe for balloon wine. It was a simple and ingenious process that I had to try immediately out of curiosity. All I needed was a gallon jug, Welch's grape juice, sugar, yeast, and a ten-cent balloon. The recipe said to put the ingredients in the jug and stretch the balloon over the opening. By the time the balloon inflated and deflated, the grape juice would be wine. Unfortunately, between the time the recipe was written and the time it came into my hands, inflation had worked its will and my balloon was too small. The pressure on the juice was so great that it exploded out of the jug all over the walls. It was an important lesson. If you are flexible and use common sense, you will experience the same joy Mamie did when she placed her food on the table for family and friends.

Standard oven temperatures are: very slow 250 degrees, slow 300 degrees, moderate 350 degrees, hot 400 degrees, very hot 450 to 500 degrees (all Fahrenheit). As ovens vary in temperature, always test cakes and ginger breads for doneness with a wooden pick until it comes out clean; test cookies by gently touching the tops until a dent is no longer left.

A Chef's Comments

History rarely or never repeats itself. Great chefs are all different, but the legacy they all leave us is a road map back in time in their recipes.

It leaves one to wonder about the countless maps that are lost forever, or only scribbled on bits and pieces of paper. Some have just enough ingredients listed to remind the chef of the flavor of the dish. Some have no instructions because the chefs wrote these recipes for themselves only. Some have ingredients listed by cost, such as in this book, when Mamie specifies "a nickel size can of Carnation cream"; at today's prices we can only guess how much cream to add. When I undertook the testing of these recipes and re-creation of the procedures, I realized that it takes a seasoned chef or someone dating back to that time to fully understand them. I could also see how the types of foods and their preparation depended on the availability of equipment and supplies.

What a beautiful story, what a frightful time it must have been to be part of the management team, to be the wife of the manager of one of the largest working ranches and to be responsible for feeding important guests and cowboys. As I began to understand how many people Mamie Burns had to please, I felt as if I were actually there and had the same responsibilities.

Mamie's recipes always left room for perhaps a secret ingredient or a pinch of this or that. All are scratch recipes that have been transcribed just as she wrote them. There is always a step or a term that only an experienced cook would be able to discern. As any good cook will tell you, after a recipe is well prepared, the

secret ingredient is always the right amount of hospitality. Great restaurants, like Mamie's table, are always
hospitable and give great service. These delicious
dishes make you want to return again and again.

Chef L. E. Anderson, CEC

A Chef's
Comments
4

Breads

$50 Cornbread

1 cup meal
3 eggs, separated
1 cup hot milk
1 heaping tsp. baking powder

1 tsp. sugar
1 Tbs. flour
1 Tbs. butter

Pour scalding milk over meal to which has been added salt, sugar, and butter. Let stand for several hours. Add flour and egg yolks. Beat egg whites lightly. Cut in. Lastly, add baking powder. This amount serves six.

Chef Anderson suggests: Use a well oiled corn bread pan and bake at 350 degrees for about 20 minutes. Or, drop by spoonfuls on a hot oiled griddle and flip over when golden. Drain on a paper towel. Serve hot.

Really worth the price!—Chef Anderson

Spoon Bread

1 pint milk	2 Tbs. butter
½ cup cornmeal	3 eggs, separated
½ tsp. baking powder	1 tsp. salt

Heat milk to boiling. Add meal, stirring until thick. Remove from stove. Add beaten yolks, baking powder, and salt. Fold in stiffly beaten whites. Turn into buttered baking dish. Bake slowly for 40 minutes.

Chef Anderson suggests: Bake in a small loaf pan or a 1-quart casserole.

Biscuits

2 cups flour	2 level tsp. baking powder
½ Tbs. soda	¾ tsp. salt
1 rounded Tbs. shortening	sour milk

Sift dry ingredients three times. Cut shortening in with fork until mealy. Add enough sour milk to make stiff paste. Roll on floured board.

Chef Anderson suggests: The sour milk Mamie used is no longer available. Substitute buttermilk for the sour milk. Pinch off pieces of dough and hand roll into a ball, then pat into biscuit shape. Let rise. Bake at 325 degrees for 20 to 25 minutes or until golden.

In the Big House, chuckhouse, or the chuck wagon our aim was large amounts of soul-satisfying foods. Foods that were hearty and comforting, hoe cakes, crackling bread, using the things we had on the place, unrationed foods. Our meals usually feature something grown in the garden. We have never surprised our guests with rattle-snake meat, although we could, nor with horned frog stew. I am told it is quite a dish. The only oddity, besides Son-Of-A-Gun, that we serve at the wagon or chuck-house, are mountain oysters, the testicles of the bull, broiled or fried—the cowman considers them quite a deli-cacy. Often listed on Western menus as "fries." We have guests to whom mountain oysters are as strange and re-pulsive fare as rattlesnake meat. We have elegance, poli-tics, and wit, and some guests who eat with their knives. It's fine.—Mamie Burns

Cheese Biscuits

2 cups flour (Swans Down)   ½ tsp. salt
2 tsp. baking powder   4 Tbs. shortening
⅔ cup milk   1 cup American
                               cheese, grated

Mix above ingredients. Roll ⅛ inch thick. Brush with melted butter. Sprinkle with cheese. Roll like jelly roll.

Chef Anderson suggests: Cut 1 ½ inch thick. Bake at 350 degrees for 20 to 25 minutes.

Light Rolls

7 cups flour	2 cups water, divided
1 yeast cake	½ cup sugar
1 egg white,	3 Tbs. shortening
stiffly beaten	1 tsp. salt

Soak yeast in ½ cup warm water. Cream sugar and shortening and salt. Add yeast and flour alternately. About half way through add stiffly beaten whites of egg. Let rise 1 ½ hours.

Chef Anderson suggests: One package of dry yeast equals 1 cake yeast. These will brown very fast because of the egg white. Bake about 5 minutes at 400 degrees.

Rolls—Three Hour

1 cup scalded milk	2 Tbs. sugar
1 tsp. salt	2 Tbs. shortening

Dissolve together and then let it get just lukewarm and crumble in one yeast cake. Mix in 2 ½ to 3 cups of flour. Let rise 2 hours. Work out and let rise for 1 hour.

Chef Anderson suggests: Bake at 350 degrees for 8 to 10 minutes.

"Work out" means to knead or work with the hands to shorten the strands of gluten in flour.—Chef Anderson

Rolls

Cream together: 1 Tbs. lard
                          1 Tbs. butter
                          1 ½ Tbs. sugar

Add: 1 egg white
                          1 cup warm milk

Dissolve 1 cake yeast in ½ cup warm water. Mix all together. Sift 1 ½ cups bread flour. Mix well and cover and let stand 1 ½ hours. Add 1 ½ cups flour and 1 ¼ tsp. salt. Knead well. Put dough in greased bowl and let rise 45 minutes. Make rolls and let rise again. Bake at 375 degrees and take out.

Chef Anderson suggests: Bake for 8 to 10 minutes or until golden.

Pitchfork Ranch Chuckhouse Rolls

6 Tbs. butter, melted in 1 cup boiling water
1 pkg. yeast dissolved in 2 Tbs. warm water
¼ cup sugar   Dash salt
1 beaten egg   3½ to 4 cups flour

Mix all ingredients except flour together well. You may use an electric beater. Add flour. Mix well. Let rise 1 ½ hours. Roll out and cut into rolls and let rise again in well buttered iron skillet putting rolls touching each other. Bake 350 degrees to golden brown. Butter tops generously while hot.

The chuck house cook told us that in the days before central heating, the cook would set the bread at night and take it to bed under the covers with him or her to help it rise by morning.—Editor

Light Bread

3 Tbs. Spry (*shortening, like Crisco*)	3 Tbsp. sugar
3 tsp. salt	2 cups milk, scald and let cool

Dissolve 1 yeast cake in ½ cup warm water and add to above. Add enough flour to make biscuit. Let rise until twice its size. Work it back, make stiff dough. Let rise again.

Chef Anderson suggests: Make into loaf or biscuits and place in greased tin. Bake at 350 degrees for 20 to 25 minutes for loaf or 10 to15 minutes for biscuits.

"Work it back" means to knead the dough or simply punch it down. Once the dough has been shaped into loaves or rolls and allowed to rise again, cooking time is approximately 12 minutes for rolls in 350-degree oven. —Chef Anderson

The hands who had their meals at the chuckhouse were fussy about the food they ate. Not in the same way as Mamie was about what she served her guests. The cowboys and other hands, then and now, keep their energy at top level with the "Three Bs," that is, Beef, Beans, and Biscuits or Bread. The chuckhouse cook told us the men weren't interested in salads, and vegetables weren't high on their list either. They were always satisfied if there was plenty of Beef, Beans and Biscuits.—Editor

Brown Bread

2 cups graham flour	1 tsp. salt	1 cup molasses
½ cup white flour	1 cup nuts	1 cup sour milk
½ cup cornmeal	1 cup raisins	1 tsp. soda
½ cup sugar	1 tsp. baking powder	
½ cup milk		

Mix molasses, sour milk and soda. Mix dry ingredients. Add nuts, raisins, and then liquids. Thin batter with ½ cup sweet milk. Bake 1 hour in buttered and floured baking powder cans. Bake slow.

Homemade Bread

2 cups warm milk	2 Tbs. sugar
2 Tbs. shortening	1 tsp. salt

Mix well. Add 1 cake yeast. Stir in 6 cups of flour and let stand 10 minutes. Knead well. Put in greased bowl for 1 ½ hours to 2 hours. Knock down. Let rise again. Knock down. Make into two parts and let rise 15 minutes. Make loaves and let rise 45 minutes. Bake in pre-heated oven 450 degrees for 5 minutes. Lower to 375 degrees to finish baking.

Waffles

2 cups flour
2 tsp. baking powder
3 eggs, separated
  and beaten

¾ tsp. salt
2 Tbs. fat
1 ½ cups sweet milk

Chef Anderson suggests: Sift dry ingredients. Beat egg white till soft peaks form. Mix egg yolk, fat, and milk together. Add dry ingredients. Fold in beaten egg whites.

These were great! A big hit on July 4th breakfast.
—*Chef Anderson*

Zola's Hot Cakes

Sift dry ingredients:

2 cups flour
2 + Tbs. sugar
4 level Tbs. baking
  powder
1 level tsp. salt

Add:

2 eggs, beaten together
2 Tbs. melted butter
1 ⅓ cups milk, warm

Chef Anderson suggests: Cook on both sides on a hot greased griddle until golden.

D liked a hearty breakfast, fruit, cereal, soft boiled eggs, bacon or pancakes and sausage, fried apples and ham, hot biscuits. A light lunch of soup and salad and time for a short nap before returning to the office.—Mamie Burns

Spiced Apple Muffins

2 ½ cups sifted flour   3 ¼ tsp. baking powder
1 tsp. salt   ½ tsp. nutmeg
¼ cup sugar   ½ tsp. cinnamon
1 egg, well beaten   ⅓ cup Spry, melted
1 ¼ cup milk   1 cup apple chopped
                              fine
2 Tbs. sugar and ¼ tsp. nutmeg sprinkled on top

Sift flour with baking powder, salt, spices, and sugar. Combine beaten egg, milk, and melted Spry. Turn liquids into dry ingredients and stir vigorously until all flour is dampened. The batter will look lumpy. Fold apples carefully into mixture.

Chef Anderson suggests: Bake at 350 degrees for 25 minutes in muffin tins.

All-Bran Muffins

2 Tbs. shortening	¼ cup sugar
1 egg	1 cup Kellogg's All-Bran
¾ cup milk	1 cup flour
½ tsp. salt	2½ tsp. baking powder

Cream shortening and sugar thoroughly. Add egg and beat well. Stir in bran and milk. Let soak until most of moisture is taken up. Sift flour with salt and baking powder. Add to first mixture and stir only until flour disappears. Fill greased muffin pan ⅔rds full and bake in oven 400 degrees about 30 minutes.

Old Fashioned Gingerbread

½ cup creamed butter	1 cup molasses
½ cup sugar	2 eggs
1 tsp. cinnamon	1 tsp. cloves
1 heaping tsp. ginger	¾ tsp. salt
1 tsp. soda	3 cups sifted flour
¾ cup hot water	

Beat sugar, shortening, eggs, and syrup together. Sift dry ingredients. Add hot water to soft ingredients. Add dry ingredients.

Chef Anderson suggests: Bake in a loaf pan (5"x9") at 325 degrees for 35 minutes.

Good!—Chef Anderson

Tropical Gingerbread

½ cup butter
½ cup sugar
2 eggs
1 tsp. cinnamon
1 tsp. salt
1 cup fresh grated
  moist coconut

1 tsp. soda
½ cup Brer Rabbit
  molasses
1 tsp. ginger
1 ½ cup flour
½ cup cold water

Cream well butter and sugar, add eggs, beat together. Dissolve soda in molasses and add to first mixture. Mix and sift remaining dry ingredients and add to first mixture alternately with cold water. Stir in coconut. Pour into well greased pan and bake in moderate oven—325 degrees for 35 minutes.

Chef Anderson suggests: Use a small loaf pan (3 ½"×7 ½"×2 ½").

Marion's Gingerbread

½ cup sugar
½ cup butter and
  lard mixed
1 ½ tsp. soda
1 tsp. ginger
1 egg, well beaten
½ tsp. salt

1 cup Brer Rabbit
  molasses
2 ½ cups flour
1 tsp. cinnamon
½ tsp. cloves
1 cup boiling water
raisins and pecans

Cream sugar and shortening, add egg, then molasses. Then dry ingredients sifted together. Add boiling water and beat! Beat!! Beat!!! Add raisins and pecans. Cook from 30 to 40 minutes in moderate oven 320 to 350 degrees.

Aunt Will (Mamie's younger sister Willie) remembers that D enjoyed making these Hoe-Cakes and eating them too. Hoe-Cakes got their name from originally being baked on the blade of a hoe. They are a small cake made of corn-meal. Aunt Will recently found this same recipe in a 1903 cookbook.—Editor

D's Hoe-Cakes

1 pint cornmeal
½ tsp. salt
boiling water

Pour enough boiling water over cornmeal to moisten it. Stir constantly and add more boiling water to make it the thickness of mush. Add the salt still stirring. Add more boiling water until batter will drop from spoon onto a hot greased griddle. Serve hot.

You can also add ½ onion, chopped, and 1 sweet pickle, chopped (⅓ cup), to make excellent Hush Puppy Hoe-Cakes.—Chef Anderson

Banana Loaf

¼ cup shortening and ½ cup sugar creamed.
Then add: 1 egg and 1 cup Kellogg's All-Bran.

Sift together: 1 ½ cup flour
                     2 tsp. baking powder
                     ½ tsp. salt
                     ½ tsp. soda.

Add ½ cup nuts.

Have ready in another bowl 1 ½ cups mashed
bananas, 2 Tbs. cold water, 1 tsp. vanilla.

Chef Anderson suggests: Mix all together and bake
in a bread pan at 325 degrees for 20 to 25 minutes.

Coffee Cake, San Angelo

2 cups sifted flour	3 tsp. baking powder
¼ cup sugar	¾ tsp. salt
¼ cup Spry	¼ cake yeast
¾ cup milk, luke warm	1 egg, well beaten

Topping:

2 Tbs. butter	1 Tbs. flour
4 Tbs. brown sugar	1 tsp. cinnamon
4 Tbs. chopped nuts	

Mix flour, sugar, salt, baking powder with Spry. Crumble yeast into warm milk. When dissolved, add to flour mixture. Add egg, well beaten, to flour mixture. Mix well. Put dough into pan greased with Spry. Sprinkle pecan topping over top and press into dough.

Chef Anderson suggests: Bake 325 degrees for 25 minutes.

This one tastes better than Sara Lee's streusel coffee cake!—Chef Anderson

The Big House at the Pitchfork Ranch. Photo courtesy of the Burns Hamilton family.

Salads, Relishes, & Condiments

Like all Gaul, our cooks and kitchens were divided into three categories. There's the chuckhouse couple, the chuck wagon cook, and there's, intermittently, the Big House couple. Cooks were the most temperamental and all-important personages on the ranch, and they knew it. Criticize one or suggest a change, and you have lost a helper.—Mamie Burns

Mamie had a series of help in the kitchens of the Big House and the chuckhouse. In her words, "they came in all colors and abilities," but her most cherished was Mandy, who worked side by side with her in the Big House.—Editor

★

Whole Tomato Salad

Select 1 large ripe tomato per person. Peel, core, salt and pepper the cavity and turn upside down to drain while chilling in the refrigerator. When ready to serve put in one dab homemade mayonnaise and pack in salsa. (Salsa: Mince 2 green peppers and 2 medium onions. Season with 2 tsp. sugar, ½ tsp. salt, 1 tsp. Worcestershire. Makes enough for 8 tomatoes.) Top with a blob of homemade mayonnaise.

Mandy ran my house a bit high-handedly, but I was glad enough to turn it over to her. "I don't work on Sunday," but on Saturdays she carefully prepared something that would be good cold for Sunday. Ham, roast chicken, tongue, some of the congealed salads she had learned to make from my cookbook, and always there would be ice cream, custards, and pound cake for dessert.—Mamie Burns

★

Neapolitan Pineapple Salad

1 pkg. lemon jello dissolved in 2 cups boiling water. Cool and add 1 large pkg. Philadelphia cream cheese (beat in) and 1 cup *whipped* cream. Pour in 12 x 4 inch Pyrex pan. Place in refrigerator until well set.

1 pkg. lime jello dissolved in 1 cup boiling water. Add juice of #2 can of Dole pineapple (crushed). Let set to shimmying stage. Whip well with rotary beater. Sprinkle well-drained pineapple over first mixture then pour over second mixture.

★

Royal Anne Cherry Salad

Pit one large can of white cherries cutting only one side for removing seed. Stuff with cream cheese softened with Kraft's mayonnaise salad dressing. Poke in half of pecan leaving top of pecan exposed. Place these in lemon jello that has been dissolved in boiling water and almost set. Chill and serve on lettuce leaf.

Fresh pineapple chunks soaked in sherry with cut up marshmallows makes a good addition to a fruit salad.—Mamie Burns

Cold Slaw with Sour Cream

3 cups finely shredded cabbage
½ cup sour cream
salt, pepper, celery seed, lemon juice

Let cabbage stand in the refrigerator in cold water most of a day. Drain well. Whip the sour cream. Add a little lemon juice and the seasoning of salt and pepper. Add a few drops of onion juice. Sprinkle with celery seeds. Serve very cold.

Sandwich Spread

Grind enough green tomatoes to make 1 quart after grinding. Drain tomatoes. Stir in 3 Tbs. salt. After a few minutes, drain, then put to cook with 1 ½ cups water. Simmer until tender and nearly dry. Add 12 sweet cucumber pickles ground.

Dressing:
5 well-beaten eggs   4 Tbs. flour
2 cups sour cream   4 Tbs. prepared
1 ½ cups vinegar   mustard

Mix together and cook until thick. Add to above while both are hot and seal.

No one ever made such a lively salad as Mandy once she became accustomed to using raw vegetables. It was her delight to add something we had not used before like turnips or pepper grass or sorrel. It pleased her to watch our expressions as the ingredients were discovered. You are apt to encounter a vegetable garden in a big wooden bowl.—Mamie Burns

Olive Oil Pickles

6 large sour pickles, cut in slices	4 cups sugar sprinkled over
4 Tbs. olive oil	1 button garlic
6 whole allspice	2 bay leaves or some pickling spices

Let oil and sugar stand in pickles for three days before jarring.

For bean dip the olive oil can make all the difference. Folks ask me for my bean dip recipe. When I come to the olive oil bit they most always say, "I prefer salad oil," though they had liked my dish well enough to ask how it was made. The same with the cheese. "I'll use Velveeta," they say instead of blue, Roquefort, etc. "We like it better." . . . well, it is cheaper.—Mamie Burns

Mother's Chow Chow

1 pkg. green tomatoes   1 large head of cabbage
½ doz. onions large or 8 small ones

Pour over above: 1 teacup salt. Mix thoroughly and let stand over night.

Drain water off, then add hot chile peppers, green and red, and 1 quart boiling water and 1 quart vinegar. Boil 15 minutes. Drain off and add 2 quarts vinegar and 4 cups sugar. Boil 15 minutes.

Chef Anderson suggests: One package tomatoes would be 4 tomatoes. Refrigerate overnight and serve cold.

Mother had a passion for cooking which neither of her daughters have inherited or absorbed. Mother thought cooking a fine art, worthy of study. Mr. Eugene [Williams, one of the owners] made me feel it was worthy of veneration. She had no jealously guarded secrets. It was one of her greatest pleasures giving her recipes. —Mamie Burns

Willie's Green Pepper Relish

2 doz. green peppers	1 doz. onions
12 hot peppers	1 quart vinegar
2 cups sugar	3 Tbs. salt

Chef Anderson suggests: Chop the peppers and onions fairly fine. Place in a pot, add sugar, vinegar, and salt and bring to a boil. Set aside until cool. Place in glass jars and seal using canning method.

Just the right touch of spice.—Chef Anderson

My sister Willie says, "Sister is so delicately constituted she must have her coffee in bed before she can heave a rock, lift a spade, or clean a chicken house." Needing coffee before I can open an eye or wiggle a toe, it seemed only thoughtful to send coffee to the rooms of my guests. This habit brings praise from some—indignation from others. Gilbert Watson had warned me the night before not to wake him with coffee at 6 o'clock in the morning, but I thought he needed that elegant eye-opening service and took it in to him (lacking any help) and had a shoe thrown near my head. I have given up the practice entirely.—Mamie Burns

Green Tomato Mince Meat

1 pkg. green tomatoes, chop and drain through
   colander 1 hour

2 lbs. brown sugar   1 ½ cup vinegar

Combine and cook until tender.

Add:

2 lbs. raisins	2 lbs. currants
½ lb. citron, chopped fine	1 Tbs. each cloves, nutmeg, allspice, and salt
½ pkg. tart apples, chopped	

Cook until comes to boil and seal using the canning method.

Chef Anderson suggests: One package tomatoes equals 4 tomatoes. Tart apples are usually small, so use 8 or 10.

Onions in White Wine

Peel 1 lb. of tiny white onions. Cover onions with dry white wine. Add 2 Tbs. of cooking oil, 1 Tbs. tomato paste, a sprig of thyme and bay leaf. Simmer very slowly until onions can be pierced. Remove onions and reduce the remaining sauce until it's the consistency of thick cream. Fish out bay leaf and thyme. Season to taste with salt and cayenne. Pour sauce back over onions and reheat and serve with poultry, fish, or game. Serve cold.

Cranberry Jelly

Four cups of berries, 1 cup water. Boil until all pop open. Mash thoroughly. Run through colander. Measure for measure of sugar and juice. Stir well.

Chef Anderson suggests: Jar and seal as for any jelly.

Mamie Burns. Photo courtesy of the Burns Hamilton family.

Meats

No meal or day was pronounced perfect unless some relative or friend shared it with us. —Mamie Burns

Liver

Liver undoubtedly has a stubborn flavor which can be improved upon by soaking it in tomato juice at least four hours before cooking. The whole process is this: Soak it, then beat it as you would for chicken fried steak with flour, salt, and pepper. Fry it a minute and a half on each side in bacon drippings. Serve with baked potato, fried onions and cabbage slaw. Of course, you fry eight slices of bacon to serve with the liver. A dish to destroy all your prejudices against liver.

One Way to Cook Beef— Pitchfork Chuckhouse Style

Use a three-inch thick cut of beef, chuck, round, or something similar. Put uncovered in a heavy pan such as a cast iron skillet or cast iron dutch oven in a 250 degree oven. Season the meat with plain salt or some garlic or onion salt and pepper. Bake uncovered for several hours until the meat is very tender. It will have turned black on the outside.

Ranch work is tough and good food is the basis for contented cowboys. At the chuckhouse we had hearty, no-fooling meals. We averaged one beef a week. Anything beyond beef, red beans, and potatoes was considered fancy. Cowboy fare must be hearty. Vegetably speaking, they'll take beans, potatoes, and tomatoes. Beans are pretty much standard fare on any ranch. We soaked ours overnight and cooked them a long, long time. What boots are to a cowboy's raiment, beans are to his stomach. With lean salt pork or ham hocks they are might tasty. They want their steaks chicken-fried and drowned in ketchup or gravy. There must be ketchup. Roast will do in a pinch, but chicken-fried steak is what the cowboys love. Ed swore, "It's got vitamins A, B, C, and D, and the gravy's got the rest of the alphabet."
—Mamie Burns

★
Steak à la Pitchfork

Prepare one large 2½-inch thick steak for each person. Have a heavy skillet hot, but not smoking. Lay the steaks in the hot skillet without fat of any kind. As one side browns, turn to brown the other side. Test for desired doneness. Cook at high heat until done, then salt and pepper. Serve on warm platter with a sprinkle of lemon juice over each or with a slice of lemon on each steak. Sprinkle of wine may be substituted for the lemon juice.

Very good—the lemon was delightful in the pan juices.—Chef Anderson

We did our bit for beef consumption by serving steaks, roasts, and hamburgers. People expect beef when they visit a ranch and were disappointed if we did not serve it. So we had steaks, two-inch steaks. D broiled them himself according to individual likes.

"This place serves the best and the prettiest steaks in this state," George Sheppard advised the other two men, as we sat down to the table. D tried to look modest. Imagine, if you can, our dismay to see those gorgeous steaks cut into inch-square bits with a peculiar looking something over them. D's consternation was evident, but before he said a word, Lucy announced, "Ah po'ed flour and water gravy on 'em. Sho makes 'em good." D couldn't say anything. He was on the verge of apoplexy.

Now the cooking of a steak is a question on which friends have been known to divide. It has even set brother against brother, Republican against Republican, Democrat against Democrat. We like ours broiled and rare, but you know there are many worthy people who don't. Cattlemen love to enliven the dinner table conversation for the benefit of strangers with subtle remarks about the good red meat. "Cripple one and run it in, D," or "That's done just enough not to hook you," or "Slide it in, turn it over, and pull it out," or "I've seen 'em get well, hurt worse than that one." Some city folk found their appetites slightly impaired by such wit. I'm in their camp.—Mamie Burns

★

Whole Roast Beef Tenderloin

The average roast beef prepared at the Pitchfork was 20 pounds and cooked rare. First it was browned thoroughly on all sides in a very hot oven or under a flame. Then the heat was lowered and the roast tested along to make sure it would be rare. It was not salted until near the end of the cooking.

Chicken Loaf

1 hen cooked and diced	salt and pepper
1 cup cooked rice	1 ½ cups bread crumbs
2 cups liquid (stock	¼ cup pimento
and milk)	3 eggs, whole

Put in loaf pan and cook in pan of hot water 1 ½ hours.

Chef Anderson suggests: Bake at 300 degrees.

Sauce for Chicken

2 cups stock and milk	1 small can
¼ cup flour	mushrooms
1 Tbs. lemon juice	¼ cup butter
chopped parsley	

Let cook until thick.

★★
Chicken Scrapple or Pressed Chicken

The basis for good scrapple is cornmeal mush with a meat of some kind and seasonings as desired, plus a broth to add a gelatin-like texture. Chicken Scrapple was a Pitchfork favorite.—Mamie Burns

Pour 4 cups boiling water in top of a double boiler. Combine 1 cup water with 1 cup cornmeal and 1 teaspoon salt. Stir this mixture until well blended, then add it gradually to the boiling water. Stir and cook until the mixture is quite thick. Have one 2-pound chicken prepared ahead by stewing it, with skin and bone removed. Reserve stock. Cut the chicken into small pieces. Combine chicken pieces with the cooked mush, with seasonings of salt, black pepper, and any other desired seasoning. Add 1 cup or a little more of the broth to the mixture and pour into large crock to set overnight, or for several hours, until it is completely congealed. It should be thick enough to cut easily. Turn out on flat surface and with a sharp knife slice into ¾-inch slices. Roll in meal and fry in hot fat. Serve very hot.

Excellent! I served this one with sliced fresh tomato salad.—Chef Anderson

Pressed chicken was one of our stand-bys. It's so quickly and easily served, but there are hours of preparation behind that "instant" delicacy! Pity those poor people who never tasted Mother's pressed chicken, not one of those sad affairs of gelatin, etc., but a scrapplelike concoction that tasted only a bit more like chicken than fish. You simply can't pin Mother down about this recipe. "It's according to the size of your hen," she says, "how much broth, cornmeal, and flour you use." One of those mother-daughter recipes handed down from generations. I do remember you start with a fat hen.—Mamie Burns

Barbecued Chicken

Fry chicken in flour as usual. Put in covered pan in slow oven for two or more hours basting with following sauce.

juice of 5 lemons	⅔ lb. butter
1 cup brown sugar	1 tsp. salt
1 tsp. each paprika and black pepper	

Sauce enough for four chickens.

Left to his own devices D's barbecue sauce suggests the hinges of Hades—so heavy handed he is with cayenne pepper and Chile pequins.—Mamie Burns

Fricassee Chicken

1 chicken	juice of ½ lemon
1 bay leaf	celery leaves or stalks
1 onion	salt and pepper

Fry chicken to golden brown. Put in baker and add: 1 Tbs. butter, 1 Tbs. bacon fat, 2 Tbs. unsalted shortening. Then add your bay leaf and onion and celery and enough boiling water to cover. Cover with tight lid, turn fire low and simmer for 1 hour. Then add the lemon juice and simmer for perhaps two more hours or until done. Can be reheated.

Chicken Chow Mein

2 3-pound chickens
2 cups diced celery
1 cup diced onions
1 #2 can Sub Gum vegetables
   (water chestnuts, bean sprouts, mushrooms,
   red peppers)
Several cups Chinese noodles

Cook chicken in cold water. Simmer slowly until tender. Skin while hot. Dice when cool. To 2 quarts of stock add all vegetables and cook until tender. Add chicken and cook ten minutes. Thicken with corn starch to gravy thickness. Serve over noodles. Serves 16 to 20.

Before guests arrive:
* *prepare cellophane bags of cut up salad greens*
* *screw-top jars for gravies, sauces, almond butter,
   and crumb butter for vegetables, especially
   over green beans, asparagus, and cauliflower
   and over fish. Also for dressing, mayonnaise,
   and French dressing.*
* *fresh pineapple chunks soaked in sherry*
* *cut up marshmallows*
* *pressed chicken or tongue*
—*Mamie Burns*

Pork Chop Chow Mein

1 lb. pork chops
½ green pepper
1 medium onion
2 tsp. LaChoy soy sauce
2 chicken bouillon cubes
salt and pepper to taste

1 cup celery
1 cup shredded
   cabbage
1 can mushrooms,
   20 cent cut up size
1 ½ cup water

Chef Anderson suggests: Brown pork chops in a wok or skillet on both sides, add vegetables and sauté about 2 to 3 minutes. Add water, soy sauce, bouillon cubes, salt and pepper to taste. Simmer. The 20-cent can of mushrooms is probably a 3–4-ounce can.

Hamburgers

1 lb. tender round steak, ground
Salt, pepper, lemon juice, Worcestershire, and bacon

Make into cakes as thick on the edges as they are in the middle. Handle lightly—exerting pressure makes them solid and dry. Wrap a piece of bacon cut in half the long way around them and skewer with tooth-pick. Have the broiler sizzling hot and brown them quickly on both sides. Lower the pan—doing them in a pan saves much washing afterwards. Cook about ten minutes. Spread with softened butter mixed with lemon juice, salt, pepper, and Worcestershire about a minute before they are done.

Really good!—Chef Anderson

Lamb in Casserole

2 meaty lamb shanks or 3 thick shoulder lamb
   chops

1 onion	4 carrots
1 cup canned tomatoes (thick)	¼ tsp. dry
1 clove of garlic, cut	ginger

Chef Anderson suggests: Place lamb in a braiser over moderate heat and brown on all sides. Add onion and continue cooking until onion is translucent. Add enough water to cover the lamb. Cover the braiser and boil for 45 minutes. Check the lamb often to be sure that the liquid has not dried out. Add more water as needed. After 45 minutes, remove the lamb and re-move braiser pan from heat. Allow the juices to settle and the excess grease will float to the top to be skimmed off and discarded. Return the lamb, defatted juices, julienne carrots, chopped onion, tomato, gin-ger, and garlic to the braiser. Cover and simmer 20 minutes longer. Season to taste with salt and pepper.

Lamb shanks are tough and require long cooking time.
—Chef Anderson

Spanish Delight

1 lb. round steak	2 medium onions
1 can corn	1 can tomato soup
1 can tomato paste	½ pkg. flat egg noodles
½ lb. American cheese, grated	

Sear meat good and brown. Fry onions. Put together and add corn, soup, tomato paste, and cook very slowly for 45 minutes. Boil noodles, butter baking dish, put layer of noodles and layer of mixture. Add grated cheese last and cook 15 or 20 minutes at 325 degrees. Will serve eight.

Chef Anderson suggests: Use ground round steak.

Chili con Carne

2 lbs. pork shoulder, coarse ground or chopped
2 lbs. rump beef, coarse ground or chopped

1 large onion	4 cloves garlic
8 large dry chiles	1 Tbs. cumin seeds
flour	salt
2 Tbs. Mexene	

Trim fat from pork shoulder. Fry fat in dutch oven. Roll meat in flour. Brown in fat. Cover and simmer while preparing chili. Clean chiles while dry. Boil in 1 quart water with chopped onion, garlic, and cumin seed. When skin is loose on chiles, put all through vegetable puree cone and pour over meat in the dutch oven. Simmer well below boiling point for 4 hours. Mix Mexene with 1 Tbs. flour and a little cold water. Thicken the gravy, let cook ½ hour. Salt if needed. Serve with plain pinto beans cooked with salt pork (*Do Not Soak Beans*) and hot tortillas and butter.

Chef Anderson suggests: Mexene is the same as chili powder.

Cowboys enjoy a hearty meal in the chuck house. Photo
courtesy of the Burns Hamilton family.

Vegetables

Succotash

#2 can lima beans	1 small can corn
1 medium sized onion	6 slices bacon
1 cup buttered bread crumbs	pepper and salt and sugar

Fry bacon crisp and save enough grease to fry onion. Add corn and let simmer ½ hour. Add beans and season. Put in 3 pieces of broken up bacon. Put in buttered casserole and sprinkle with crumbs and extra bacon. Let work a few minutes. Serves 8.

Chef Anderson suggests: Place in a 350- to 400-degree oven and bake until bread crumbs are golden brown and the casserole is bubbly.

★

Fried Corn

Not many know how to prepare corn to be fried in a skillet. The secret lies in the cutting of the corn from the cob. One must have the corn shucked and silked. With a very sharp knife, just barely tip the grains from one end of the ear to the other. Come back the second time and cut just a bit more from the grains. Then scrape clear down to the cob for the sweet milk.

As everyone who has had the joy of going to the corn patch for his own roasting ears knows, there is a very short period when the ear is just right for eating. The kernels must not be too tender—those are blisters—and not too hard, or the corn will have lost its tastiness and flavor. The grains should be round and full, bursting with sweet milk that pours out when pierced by the thumbnail. I, like Mandy, "don't confidence them as goes into the patch pulling ears ever' whichaways." First you look for an ear topped by a coarse, dry, brown hair-like substance called the silk. You have to strip the shuck down just enough to see and puncture a grain before you can be sure. This perfect stage lasts just about an hour according to Mandy, and she's the one who had to "pull 'em 'cause Miz Burns'll be on the telephone and Jeet'd never get there in time."—Mamie Burns

★ ★
Baked Grits

Long before the Carters made grits well known the Pitchfork served the following:
—Mamie Burns

To make about 25 servings, cook and salt 4 cups grits according to package directions. Just before removing them from the heat add ½ cup butter, ⅓ cup bacon fat, 5 eggs, and 2 cups grated sharp cheese. Stir well then fold in 2 to 4 tablespoons minced jalapeno peppers, or according to taste. Pour into a well-buttered casserole or baking pan and bake at 400 degrees for about 30 minutes or until slightly brown. Cut into squares or slices and serve very hot.

★
Baked Potato

A potato baked to mealiness popped open just enough to allow a spoon of thick cream, pepper and salt, and a sprinkling of paprika. No microwaves and no aluminum foil to steam the potatoes into soap-like hardness.—Mamie Burns

D and Mamie encourage their grandchildren Burns and Anne to read. Photo courtesy of *The Cotton Gin and Oil Mill Press.*

Desserts

Holland Rusk Dessert

Custard

2 cups milk	4 egg yolks
1 Tbs. corn starch, slightly rounded	½ cup sugar

Cook over low heat, stirring, until thickened. Let cool while making crust.

Crust

1 box zwieback rolled fine. Mix ½ cup sugar into it. Butter pie plate generously and press ½ mixture into it. Pour in custard. Beat egg whites with 4 Tbs. sugar. Cover custard with egg whites and add chopped nuts to remainder of zwieback and sprinkle over top. Bake 45 minutes at 350 degrees. Serve cold.

Deep-Dish Peach Cobbler

Mix together ½ cup melted butter, ½ cup sugar, ½ cup milk, ½ cup flour, and 1 teaspoon baking powder. Stir until smooth. Pour the batter into a baking dish or pan, add 4 cups sweetened fresh peaches, but do not stir. (Frozen peaches may be substituted.) Bake in a 375 degree oven for about 30 minutes, or until the batter comes to the top and is browned. Ice cream or whipped cream may be served over each helping.

★
Crème Brûlée

This was the favorite and the most elegant of the Pitch-fork's desserts. It was served often and always appreciated. —Mamie Burns

Heat 2 cups cream in a double boiler. Beat 4 egg yolks, adding 3 tablespoons sugar gradually. Remove cream from heat and pour very slowly over the beaten eggs. Add 1 teaspoon vanilla and pour into a 1 ½-quart casserole, place in a pan of hot water and bake uncovered at 325 degrees for about 45 minutes or until well set. Sprinkle ⅓ cup brown sugar over the top and place under the broiler until sugar melts. Chill and serve very cold spooned over fresh fruit poached in heavy syrup—half pears or half peaches, for instance.

Excellent! Very rich and satisfying. —Chef Anderson

I always sat at the foot of the dining room table with the kitchen immediately behind me. D sat at the head, so it was he who most often registered surprise or consternation at what was coming through the swinging door. His startled expressions have alerted me more than once to approaching catastrophe. Sometimes it was amusement in his wicked eyes. Such was the case when Rose, the Indian girl, appeared to serve dessert, wearing one of my dresses, and a very good dress, I might add. She explained that she had spilled beet juice down the front of her uniform and it was raining. "More better wear your dress than get wet going to my house." Perhaps, but if she had spilled crème brûlée down the front of that dress, more better she leave. —Mamie Burns

★

Custard—Basic

3 eggs	2 cups milk
⅔ cup sugar	2 Tbs. flour
dash salt	½ tsp. vanilla
butter	

Blend flour, sugar, salt, and eggs. Heat milk and butter on stove until scalded. While stirring, add liquid to the egg mixture stirring until smooth. Add vanilla. Pour into an earthenware dish. Set the dish in a shallow pan and pour water ⅓ up the side of the dish. Bake at 350 degrees for 35 minutes.

Chef Anderson suggests: Use 2 Tbs. butter. Cream or Half and Half may be substituted for milk for a richer custard. Bake in a Pyrex 9" or 10" pie or cake pan.

Willie's German Lizzies

2 cups brown sugar
1 ½ lbs. mixed fruits
　(raisins, citron, cherries,
　pineapple)
½ lb. chopped nuts
3 tsp. soda
1 glass whiskey
1 tsp. nutmeg

½ cup butter
4 eggs beaten
　together
3 Tbs. sweet
　milk
1 tsp. cinnamon
3 cups flour

Cream butter and sugar, add well-beaten eggs. Toss the fruit in a small amount of flour and add. Sift flour with soda and spices and add alternately with whiskey and milk. Drop on greased cookie sheet and bake in slow oven.

Chef Anderson suggests: One glass of whiskey is about 2 ounces.

Glazed Pecan Cookies

1 cup butter
1 cup sugar
} cream together

Add yolk of one egg
Add 2 ½ cups of flour with 1 tsp. cinnamon

Beat egg white lightly and spread on cookies that are spread thinly on cookie sheet. Sprinkle with 1 cup finely chopped nuts. Press in firmly. Cook in moderate oven.

Brownies

2 cups sugar
1 cup melted butter
4 eggs, beaten whole
2 cups nuts
1 tsp. vanilla

pinch of salt
½ of a large cake
   Bakers Chocolate
2 cups bread flour

Melt chocolate with butter. Mix in order given. Bake in large pan in a moderate oven for about 20 minutes. Remove from oven and cut into long sticks while hot. When cold, take from pan. Keep well.

Very good.—Chef Anderson

Corn Flakes Cookies

4 egg whites
1 cup sugar
1 cup pecans
1 cup dry coconut

3 cups corn flakes, toasted
   slightly
1 tsp. vanilla

Beat whites rather stiff, add sugar and other ingredients. Drop on greased tin. Cook slowly.

Ground Nut Cookies

2 cups brown sugar
2 eggs, separated

2 cups nuts thoroughly
    chopped

Mix yolks with sugar and nuts. Add beaten whites. Drop on buttered tin and cook very slowly at 200 degrees.

Fudge Squares

Melt 8 Tbs. cocoa in ½ cup butter. Add 1 cup sugar slowly to 3 slightly beaten eggs. Add cocoa mixture. Add ¾ cup flour with ½ tsp. salt, ½ tsp. baking powder, ½ tsp. vanilla, and 1 cup nuts floured in part of the flour. Bake in moderate oven. Do *not* cook until done.

Chef Anderson suggests: Use a 9"×9" pan and test with wooden pick after 30–35 minutes. Pick should show cookies to be slightly sticky.

Peanut Butter Cookies

1 cup white sugar
1 cup peanut butter
2 eggs, well beaten
1 tsp. baking powder
½ tsp. salt

1 cup brown sugar
1 cup butter
2½ cups flour
½ tsp. soda
½ tsp. vanilla

Chef Anderson suggests: Mix together and drop by spoonfuls on cookie sheet. Press down tops with a fork. Bake in a 300-degree oven for 20 minutes.

Sand Tarts

1 cup butter and 1 cup nuts, ground. Work thoroughly together and then add 3 Tbs. powdered sugar and 1 tsp. vanilla. Pile 2 cups unsifted flour on board and pour first mixture in center. Work in. Make into roll. Cut in small slices and roll into balls. Bake in 375 oven about 20 minutes. Do not brown. Let cool. Before using, put powdered sugar in sack and carefully shake cookies in sugar. Later sift sugar over again. Makes about 30 cookies or 40.

Vida's Lemon Ice Cream

Juice of 5 lemons and 2 cups sugar mixed together. Whip 1 pint of cream lightly. Mix lemon juice and sugar very slowly into cream. Add whole milk up to amount needed.

Chef Anderson suggests: Makes 2 quarts. Proceed to freeze as for your ice cream freezer directions.

Lemon Ice Cream

2 eggs, beaten. Add ½ cup sugar. Add ½ cup corn syrup (white), 2 tsp. grated lemon rind, ¼ cup lemon juice, 2 cups cream (whipped). Fast freeze for 1 hour and reduce temperature.

You can't find this delightful ice cream in stores any more. Too bad!—Chef Anderson

Milky Way Ice Cream

2 Milky Way candy bars   ½ cup milk

Heat milk, put candy in milk until it melts. Cool and fold in 1 cup of cream, whipped. Freeze.

Bund Kuchen

1 cup butter, creamed with 2 cups sugar, sifted
5 eggs, one at a time beaten in
2 tsp. baking powder
3½ cups flour, sifted 5 times   pinch salt
rind of 1 lemon   rind of 1 orange
1 cup milk added alternately   ½ cup pecans
   with flour and baking powder

Add one egg at a time and beat after every addition. Cook in pan well greased and floured with pecans pressed into the sides. Cook 1 hour and 25 minutes at 325 degrees.

Chef Anderson suggests: Bake this kuchen in a cake pan or a loaf pan.

Desserts
53

Special Fudge Cake

½ cup Spry
2 cups brown sugar
2 large eggs
2 cups flour
1 tsp. soda

½ tsp. salt
½ cup sour milk
½ cup water
6 Tbs. cocoa
1 tsp. vanilla

Cream shortening first, add sugar gradually and cream well. Blend in the well-beaten eggs. Sift flour once before measuring then sift flour, soda, and salt together and add to the creamed mixture alternately with the sour milk and water. Blend in cocoa and vanilla. Pour into two well-greased and floured pans. Bake 30 to 35 minutes at 350 degrees. When cooled, spread icing between layers and over the top and sides of the cake. Always pack brown sugar down well in cup.

Brown Sugar Marshmallow Nut Icing

2 cups brown sugar
½ cup milk
½ cup chopped nuts

12 large marshmallows,
cut in small pieces
¼ cup butter

Boil sugar and milk together slowly without stirring to soft ball stage. Keep pan covered during first three minutes to prevent crystals forming on sides of pan. Remove from heat, add butter and marshmallows. When mixture is cool, beat until creamy. Add nuts and beat until right consistency to spread. To thin, add cream ½ tsp. at a time.

Duchess Cupcakes

½ cup butter
1½ cups brown sugar
2 eggs
1 cup thick sour milk
   or buttermilk
2 cups cake flour,
   sifted before measuring
¼ tsp. salt

1 tsp. soda
1 tsp. cinnamon
½ tsp. cloves
½ tsp. nutmeg
½ cup broken nut
   meats

Cream butter, add sugar gradually, beat until fluffy. Add eggs, one at a time, beating after addition of each. Sift flour with soda and spices. Add alternately with sour milk to the first mixture. Mix nuts with last addition of flour. Turn into paper baking cups, fill about ½ full and place on a shallow pan or baking sheet. Temperature—425 degrees. Baking time—10 minutes for small cakes, 15 minutes for large cakes. Makes 48 small cakes or 24 large cakes.

Sour Cream Pound Cake

Juanell Tubbs was very ill and I, being a good Lubbock neighbor, took this pound cake to her. Later that evening her husband Fenner called me. "Where did you get Mamie Burns's recipe?!! I haven't eaten that cake since going out to the ranch hunting with D a long time ago. Seems every time I was there Mamie had coffee and this cake waiting for us when we came in."—Editor

On the ranch we catered to men and this pound cake recipe is one that men particularly like. It stays moist for as long as you can keep it around.—Mamie Burns

Cream together two sticks margarine and 2 cups sugar. Sift 2 cups cake flour with ¼ tsp. salt. Add to butter mixture. Add 3 eggs, one at a time, beating well after each addition. Add 1 cup sour cream, 2 tsp. vanilla. Bake in greased and floured tube pan for 1 hour at 350 degrees. Add the following glaze while still warm, but not hot. Mix ½ stick butter melted, 2 Tbs. lemon juice, and 1 cup sifted powdered sugar.

Frozen Fruit Cake

2 cups almond macaroons broken into small pieces
1 cup pecans   1 cup chopped white raisins
¼ cup flour   2 cups milk
½ cup sugar   1 cup whipped cream
2 eggs   cheese glass of whiskey

Scald milk and add sugar, flour, macaroons, raisins. Cool 10 minutes. Stir and add eggs, whiskey, pecans, and whipped cream. Freeze.

The whiskey will cook the eggs.—Chef Anderson

However, the whiskey will not kill bacteria as heat will. Therefore, be sure your eggs are fresh and with no cracks.—Editor

El's Fruit Cake

6 eggs, beaten together   1 lb. sugar (2 cups)
1 lb. flour (4 cups)   2 heaping tsp. baking
¾ lb. butter   powder
2 lbs. chopped fruit   1 lb. pecans
1 lb. raisins   1 tsp. grated nutmeg
1 cup whiskey   ½ cup molasses
½ cup grated orange peel

Chef Anderson suggests: Cream sugar and butter, add eggs, well beaten. Add flour and liquid alternately. Flour raisins, candied fruit, and nuts and add last. Bake or steam in a standard 2 quart bread pan. You may steam this fruit cake for about 3 hours. Or bake at 300 degrees. Test after 1 ½ hours to see if pick comes out dry.

White Cake Filling

2 level Tbs. Snow Drift   ½ pint of cream
about 1 ½ boxes of
   powdered sugar
Beat cream thoroughly when adding to sugar.

Chef Anderson suggests: Add more sugar if needed. This will not be thick.

Snow Drift is a stabilizer that keeps cream and sugar, especially whipped cream, from separating. Snow Drift is no longer available but Meringue Powder may be used and can be found at craft stores or cake decorating shops.—Editor

One Egg Cake

¼ cup shortening   ½ cup milk or water
1 cup sugar   1 egg
1 ½ cup flour   2 tsp. baking powder

Cream sugar and shortening, add water or milk alternately with flour sifted with baking powder. Stir in egg. Bake in two layers.

Chef Anderson suggests: Bake in greased and floured pans at 350 degrees for 20 to 25 minutes.

Pie Crust

1 ½ cup flour   ½ cup shortening
½ tsp. salt   3 to 4 Tbs. ice water

Sift flour once before measuring and sift flour and salt together. Cut in shortening with two knives or pastry blender, leaving some of the Spry in lumps the size of giant peas.

Sprinkle the ice water lightly, a little at a time, over flour and shortening. At first blend gently with a fork, then gather the dough together lightly with fingertips. As soon as you can make it stick together, round up the dough on a cloth-covered board with flour rubbed into the cloth to keep dough from sticking. Divide the dough into half and roll out one half to fit the pie pan loosely, without stretching. Be sure to leave pan on table while cutting off extra pastry. Chill thoroughly. Fill with pie filling and top with other half of crust. Bake as usual.

Magic Lemon Meringue Pie

1 can Eagle Brand Magic milk   ½ cup lemon juice
grated rind of 1 lemon   2 eggs separated
2 Tbs. granulated sugar

Blend together the milk, lemon juice, lemon rind, and egg yolks. Pour into baked pie shell. Cover with meringue made by beating whites until stiff and adding sugar. Bake in moderate oven 350 degrees for 10 minutes or until brown. Chill before serving.

Willie's Best Old Fashioned Lemon Pie

¼ cup lemon juice   1 cup sugar
2 whole eggs plus 2 egg yolks   ½ cup butter

Put into double boiler and let get to pie consistency. Chill. Pour into baked pie shell. Beat egg whites and add 2 Tbs. sugar to stiff peaks. Cover filling with whipped whites. Run into hot oven and brown. Let cool and serve. Serves 6 to 8.

This one is great!—Chef Anderson

Syrup Crumb Pie

¾ cup seedless raisins   3 eggs
1 ½ cup maple syrup   1 ¼ cup graham cracker
⅓ cup flour   or cracker crumbs
¼ tsp. nutmeg   1 ½ tsp. cinnamon
⅓ cup butter   ¼ tsp. ginger
¼ tsp. salt   ⅓ cup sugar
                                            ½ tsp. vanilla

Line 9-inch pie pan with pastry. Sprinkle raisins over bottom. Beat egg yolks and add syrup and pour over raisins. Combine crumbs, flour, spices, and butter. Work together thoroughly and sprinkle over top of pie. Bake 15 minutes or until crust is lightly browned in hot oven 450 degrees. Reduce heat to 325 degrees and bake 20 minutes or until pie is set.

Molasses Pie

4 eggs, beaten separately   1 cup sugar, add to
1 lb. butter   yolks
1 pinch of nutmeg   1 ½ cup molasses

Chef Anderson suggests: Line 9-inch pie pan with pastry. Pour mixture into pie shell. Cook in slow oven at 300 degrees for 45 minutes.

Burns and Anne were Mamie's grandchildren who lived on the ranch with Mamie and D.—Editor

There were Connecticut friends visiting who lived in a House and Garden *home with antiques and family retainers, so my best silver and linen were brought out for the first time in ages. Burns slid into his chair beside Anne, spied his napkin, placed his hands to his mouth, and in the loudest stage whisper ever said, "Look, Anne, rag napkins!" Our diplomatic guest smiled, "Burns, it's been a long time since our home has known the pleasure of rag napkins."—Mamie Burns*

Willie's Ambassador B B Pie

Make special dark crust. When cooked, fill with layer of chocolate custard, layer of fluffy rum flavored custard, top with whipped cream and garnish with shaved chocolate. Chill thoroughly before serving.

Crust: 16 large sized ginger cookies or 32 small sized ones and 5 Tbs. melted butter. Roll cookies fine, add melted butter and mix well. Place in 9 inch pie tin. Arrange in pie crust form and bake 10 minutes in slow oven 300 degrees.

Filling: 1 1/3 Tbs. gelatin, 2 cups milk, 4 tsp. cold water, 1/2 cup sugar, 1 1/4 tsp. corn starch, 4 egg yolks.

Chocolate Custard Layer: 1 1/2 squares bitter chocolate melted and 1 Tbs. vanilla.

Rum Flavored Layer: 4 egg whites, 1/2 cup sugar, 1/4 tsp. cream of tartar, 1 tsp. lemon extract, 1 tsp. vanilla extract.

Topping: 1 cup cream, whipped, 2 tsp. confectioners sugar, 1/2 square shaved chocolate.

Method: Soak gelatin in cold water, scald milk, combine sugar and corn starch. Beat egg yolks, add scalded milk slowly, then stir in sugar and corn starch Cook over simmering water stirring occasionally for 20 minutes or until custard coats a spoon. Remove from heat and add gelatin. Take out 1 cup of custard, to this add melted chocolate and heat until thickens. When cool add vanilla and pour into cooled crust and chill.

Take remaining custard and cook and thicken (do not allow to stiffen). Make a stiff meringue by beating egg whites until frothy, add cream of tartar and beat whites until stiff enough to hold a point. Then gradually beat in sugar until *very* stiff. Fold custard into meringue and blend in flavoring.

As soon as chocolate layer has begun to set, cover it with the fluffy rum custard and chill.

After this sets, spread with the whipped cream sweetened with confectioners sugar. Sprinkle grated chocolate over and chill thoroughly before serving.

"Rag napkin" quality. I have had this pie before by the name of Black Bottom Pie!—Chef Anderson

"World Round" Fudge

2 cups sugar	1 cup cream
2 Tbs. cocoa	butter size of walnut
dash of salt	

Cook until good soft ball. Put in three containers to cool. Beat and beat and beat . . .

Pralines

1 cup brown sugar
5 Tbs. water
pinch of salt

1 cup white sugar
1 Tbs. butter

Cook until soft ball stage. Beat until *certain* consistency. Add nuts.

Chef Anderson suggests: That "certain" consistency is when the mixture becomes stiff and chalky in appearance. Then drop by spoonfuls on wax paper.

Cream Pralines

2 cups sugar
2 cups pecans

1 can Carnation cream, 5 cents
pinch salt

Chef Anderson suggests: Cook the sugar and cream until it boils and becomes a caramel consistency. Remove from heat. Add salt and pecans. Beat while hot. Spoon onto greased sheet to cool. A 5-cent can of cream would be a 5-ounce can.

Mamie arranges festive snacks at Christmas. Photo courtesy of the Burns Hamilton family.

Beverages

Willie's Egg Nog

8 eggs, yolks and whites beaten separately
1 ¼+ cup sugar
1 quart whipping cream   ½ pint whiskey

Beat egg yolks, add 1 ¼ plus cups sugar and beat until white. Add slowly all of the whiskey. Take 1 cup sugar and ¼ cup of water and cook until not quite threading. Pour over stiffly beaten whites and add beaten cream.

Chef Anderson suggests: Combine, chill, serve in large bowl.

To avoid bacterial contamination, be sure your eggs are fresh and have no cracks.—Editor

Ginger Ale Punch

1 ½ cup sugar
¼ cup mint leaves
2 quarts iced water

1 cup water
1 cup lemon juice
1 quart iced ginger ale

Mix sugar and 1 cup water and boil three minutes. Add mint leaves, then cool. Add lemon juice and water. Last of all add ginger ale just before serving.

Good!!—Chef Anderson

Miscellaneous

Hors d'Oeuvres

Boil three eggs hard. Cut lengthwise, remove yolks. Devil yolks with pepper, salt, pinch of sugar, 1 tsp. Worcestershire sauce, 1 tsp. each of soft butter and French dressing, a half tsp. anchovy paste. Mix to a creamy paste and refill the egg whites. Remove six shrimp from glass jar and with a sharp knife split them down the curved side, but not clear through. Set them to marinate in a little French dressing to which the juice of an onion has been added for half an hour. Cut small circles of brioche. Toast on one side, brush over the other side lightly with anchovy paste. Drain the shrimp, lay on evenly and place the egg on top. Put fine lace paper doily on small plates to serve.

Shrimp Bisque

Mix 3 cans frozen shrimp soup, 2 cans frozen oyster stew, 1 quart milk, 1/3 tsp. mace, 1 Tbs. minced onion, 1 can of tiny shrimp, drained. Heat and add 1 cup sherry before serving. Serves 12.

Chuck Wagon Coffee

"There was a time," says a Marlboro cigarette ad, "when the only chuck wagon around was the long-eared kind, one mule carrying a chuck box full of food." Then in 1866, Charles Goodnight took that chuck box and put four mules in front of it, four wheels under it, and a cantankerous old cook to look after it. The chuck wagon became, as one of our cowboys said, "Home in the middle of nowhere."

Cowboys have nothing but contempt for a cook who is just a cook. Only a well-seasoned cowhand-turned-cook has the proper sense of timing to understand why they are hours late for a meal sometimes and will keep the food hot and ready. A wagon cook must be adept at improvising camp, throwing up a tarpaulin for shade in summer or rigging it up as a windbreak so he can cook in a norther or a driving rain. These simple and homely tasks require a certain amount of knowledge.

Coffee is the first thing on the fire at the cook's roll-out long before day, and throughout the day and night. The old-time wagon cook used to tell the tenderfoot his recipe for making cowboy coffee. With the greatest of secrecy he'd say, "Well now you take two pounds of Arbuckle, put in enough water to wet it down, boil for two hours, then throw in a hoss shoe. If the hoss shoe sinks, she ain't done." The cowman likes his coffee to kick up in the middle and pack double.—Mamie Burns

The whole family gathers for a Christmas celebration at the Big House. Left to right: Willie McGuire (Mamie's sister), Gordon McGuire, Anne Hamilton, Burns Hamilton, D and Mamie Burns (standing), Anne McGuire Simmons, Annie Sypert (Mamie's mother), Charlie Simmons, James Sypert (Mamie's father). Photo courtesy of the Burns Hamilton family.

Menus & Special Occasions

La Fonda Menu

Mamie visited the famous La Fonda restaurant and was so taken with the food that she requested the recipes. The cook couldn't refuse Mamie.—Editor

Huacamole & Tostadas

Remove meat of very ripe avocado from shells and mash with fork. Season to taste with chopped onion, lemon juice, salt, and Tabasco sauce. Serve in crisp lettuce nest.

With the above, serve crisply fried tortillas and dip these tostadas into the paste to eat.

Breast of Chicken Lucrecio

Cut a 5-pound hen in serving pieces. Place in deep kettle and entirely cover with hot water. Season with 1 Tbs. mixed pickling spice. Bring water slowly to boiling, reduce heat and simmer about 2½ hours. Remove breast and roll it in a mixture of ⅓ cup chili powder and ⅔ cup of flour. Fry in shallow fat until golden brown. Make a gravy by adding flour to the fat and gradually adding chicken stock. Return chicken breast to pan and let simmer about 20 minutes stirring gravy frequently. Pour gravy over the hot chicken breast on platter.

While chicken is simmering, blanch ¼ lb. almonds, chop coarsely, brown in butter and sprinkle over chicken just before serving. Serves 4. Chicken legs may be used the same way.

Use the "rag napkins" on this one!—Chef Anderson

Posole

½ lb. lean pork, diced	1 Tbs. salad oil
2 cups hominy, drained	1 tsp. salt
⅛ tsp. pepper	

Brown pork in hot salad oil. Cover and simmer until tender. Add hominy seasoned with salt and pepper. Cook 20 minutes. Serves 4.

Chef Anderson suggests: Use canned or cooked hominy. Drain before using.

Catchy! There is magic in the name alone.—Chef Anderson

Salsa

Shred: 2 green peppers and 2 medium onions

Season with: 2 tsp. sugar and ½ tsp. salt

Chill: 4 whole well-drained canned tomatoes

Arrange on lettuce leaf and fill tomatoes with mixture. Serves 4.

Chef Anderson suggests: Top with mayonnaise and a sprinkle of paprika.

Good Old Stand-By Menu

Whole Roast Beef Tenderloin—about 20 pounds
Wild Rice
Stuffed Tomato Salad
Spinach or Broccoli Soufflé
Toast Strips or Rolls
Crème Brûlée

The Christmas Cake

There was a favorite white cake that the whole family had to be involved in to make. Unfortunately when my great-grandmother passed away she held some keys that no one else remembered.

This cake took days to make with help from Gagoo (my great-grandmother), Mamie (my grandmother), Aunt Will (my great aunt), and Alzeda (Aunt Will's maid). This cake was made only at Christmas since that was the only time everyone got together with time enough to do what it took to make this cake. Gagoo called it her "lots of eggs cake."

Now!! This cake was a white three-layer cake that was light as a feather. Between the layers was a very thin coating of what I would guess would be the same as the icing (pure whipped cream and pecans with maybe a touch of sugar). After it was iced, a sprinkling of grated coconut covered the entire surface. Sounds pretty plain jane, doesn't it—IT WASN'T!!!

This was not served at breakfast/brunch.—Grandson Burns Hamilton

Christmas Breakfast/Brunch

Our family Christmas was always a large gathering which included moms, dads, aunts, uncles, grands, great grands, and all of the kiddos.

We alternated locations between the Pitchfork and Aunt Will's house in Lamesa but the agenda was pretty much the same.

Everyone got up early and the men went hunting and the women began preparing the magnificent breakfast of fried dove, fried quail, biscuit, fried sausage, pressed chicken, and everyone's favorite, eggnog.

Since it was in the middle of hunting season, fresh dove and quail were always available at Christmas. The sausage came from the Pitchfork and had been personally flavored and smoked by D Burns. According to the cowboys he made three flavors: hot, hotter, and hot as hell. Pressed chicken was a rather unusual concoction of cornmeal, broth, and boned chicken molded into bricks and fried. A real family favorite.

This was not your normal eggnog you poured into a cup or mug. It had to be served by spoon. It was made from fresh whipped cream, raw eggs, sugar, and just enough Canadian Club to make it perfect.

This was a breakfast no one will ever forget and it made Christmas morning very special!—Grandson Burns Hamilton

Chuckhouse Fare

In the chuckhouse there were always big breakfasts, dinners, and suppers—hardly any difference between the size and quality of the meals. There was an assortment of dry cereals and perhaps a cooked one; hot biscuits; ham, bacon, sausage (always two meats); jellies or dried fruit, apples, raisins, prunes.

At noon we had at least four vegetables: corn, beans, blackeyed peas, potatoes, onions, tomatoes, and anything else that might be growing in the garden. Meats were generally chicken fried steak, roast, meatloaf, ham, backbone spare ribs. Almost always chicken on Sundays. The boys liked fried best, but sometimes there would be baked hen and dressing. Salads were cold slaw, mixed greens with bacon drippings, cucumbers and onions sliced in vinegar. The men were notoriously partial to potato salad with hard boiled eggs and pickles mixed into it.

Three kinds of desserts were standard: cake, pies, puddings, jello, or cobblers and always ice cream. The men went to the dessert table for their own helpings and they always came away with two big dips of ice cream.— Mamie Burns

To learn more about the Pitchfork Ranch and Mamie and D Burns, see the following:

This I Can Leave You by Mamie Sypert Burns. College Station: Texas A & M Press, 1986. These are the stories Mamie wrote about her years on the Pitchfork giving insight into the lives of the cowboys, ranch hands, and those who lived in the Big House.

Pitchfork Land and Cattle Company: The First Century by David J. Murrah. Guthrie, Texas: Pitchfork Land and Cattle Company, 1983. This is a brief history of the Pitchfork Ranch.

Pitchfork Country: The Photography of Bob Moorhouse with text by Jim Pfluger, foreword by Wyman Meinzer. Lubbock: National Ranching Heritage Center, Texas Tech University, 2000. Bob Moorhouse is the current manager of the Pitchfork Ranch and is an accomplished photographer.

The Pitchfork Ranch also has an extensive web site.

78

Index

A

All-Bran Muffins, 14

B

Baked Grits, 43
Baked Potato, 44
Banana Loaf, 17
Barbecued Chicken, 34
Biscuits, 6
Breast of Chicken Lucrecio, 72
Brown Bread, 11
Brown Sugar Marshmallow Nut Icing, 54
Brownies, 50
Bund Kuchen, 53

C

Cheese Biscuits, 7
Chicken Chow Mein, 36
Chicken Loaf, 32
Chicken Scrapple or Pressed Chicken, 33
Chili con Carne, 40
Christmas Breakfast/Brunch, 75
Christmas Cake, 74
Chuck Wagon Coffee, 69
Chuckhouse Fare, 76
Coffee Cake, San Angelo, 18
Cold Slaw with Sour Cream, 22
Corn Flakes Cookies, 50
Cranberry Jelly, 27
Cream Pralines, 64
Crème Brûlée, 47
Custard—Basic, 48

S

T

V

W